D1477494

TRIADA

Heroes of the Teton Mythos

Solstice West from Tao

Longhair

Sam Hamill's
TRIADA

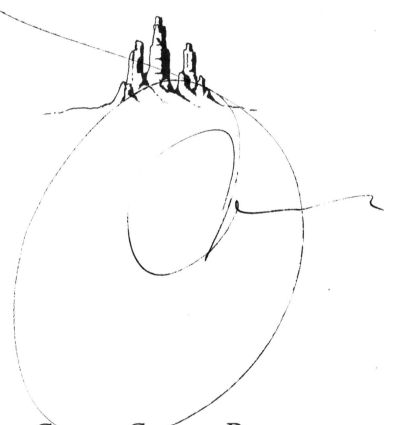

Copper Canyon Press

Early drafts of fragments of this poem appeared in the periodicals "Invisible City" and "Spectrum," and in the following books : 20 *Times in the Same Place* (Painted Cave Books), *Heroes of the Teton Mythos* (Copper Canyon Press), *Uintah Blue* (Copper Canyon Press), and *Petroglyphs* (Three Rivers Press).

Special thanks to the following : Joseph F. Wheeler and Centrum Foundation, Port Townsend, Washington, where Copper Canyon is press-in-residence ; and to the National Endowment for the Arts, a federal agency, for financial assistance to the press which, in part, made possible publication of this and other books.

Copper Canyon Press, Box 271, Port Townsend, Wa. 98368

This poem is for

TREE

and for my mother
and to the memory of my father
Sam B. Hamill Jr.
1903—1976
who gave me both name and place when I had none

BOOK ONE

Heroes of the Teton Mythos

I

Pushing up the ice floe,
early winter ice
folding at the bow,
a soft chug-a-lug, chug-a-lug,
before the motors stop.

Like mourners, like churchmen,
parkas zipperd & snapt,
hoods, furcollars rippling in the wind,
they file out, singly,
        across the ice,
dark Franciscans from nowhere
now at the end of the earth.

The file collapses, bodies
move upwind and down
        in silence,
in slow motion,
each toward a white pufft head,
each toward wide eyes bobbing in blubber.

In unison, almost,

like cops,
they raise their clubs.
It is the weather of the Virgin,
weather of purity
veiling the North in celibate white,
    white on white,
washing the wind of all bloodscent.

    "It's cold.
    The wind blows.
    It starts snowing.
    You try to get seals.

    The club freezes in your hands,
    gets heavy.
    You aim & miss. You aim
    again, hit.
    It starts wailing.
    The wind blows snow in your face.
    You hit three, four times.
    You're sure it's dead.
    You turn it.
    You turn it,
    open it, start
    tearing the skin off.
    Suddenly, it
    rolls its eyes
    & screams."

For love of myself I stript myself
of its skin,
    leaving her the memory
    to wrap herself in.

10

Now in the endless bed
it is twilight for months on end,
the winds careen across the skull
    my wits are claspt in,
my limbs are useless, but my eyes,
my eyes go on seeing.

Drifting into the waterway my life shall be
the sweet seabreath thickens,
lungs grind to a standstill :
I will forever dream words I can crawl inside.
How many, the desolate nights I walkt the beach
& watcht the fog come lumbering in?
I think it is steam
rising from dungpiles
    through falling snow
near my father's chicken coops.
Or the dapple mare's
    steamy breath,
her rump to the wind in steep snow,
fat, fatter, with foal.

It is always better in time, the cold
not quite so bitter.
Like weathering it all on film.
How young I was
when, in light of half-moon,
I took a bit of hose, a flashlight,
and entered the coop
swiftly as silence filling the dead.
A hundred hens cluckt softly,
dreaming of egg or of ax.
Peeling back each bale

I splatterd mice across the concrete wall
& left them, trophies for cats in a feed bin.
I will be Hemingway!
I'll live by the gun and worship the hunt!

The Old Man has it
the moon shines still
on that tacky ground
beneath the bones of a plum tree
from which he, years ago,
hung three hens by their heels
and opened their throats with a boning knife.

May, the mare foaled,
but the colt was turned. & the Old Man
plunged into her sex to the elbow
and tore the runt from her womb.

I rode that little horse
through old badlands
wearing sealskin gloves,
snakeskin belt, and kangaroo boots.
& years later, lost in that hawkweed wild,
I rolled a smoke in an old adobe cell
and watcht the shot-gunned stars
through a barred, open ceiling,
my tenuous footpaths swallowed by the sand.

It was a country of cracked cups,
        of coffee stains.
A country of tonguebones rattling broken teeth
where tendrils stand skinny of vine,
a land

of busted backs and Bull Durham sacks,
rattlers lolling in disused skulls,
lizards among ribs,
where dead men roamed sunblind in circles,
too dumb, too numb, to lie down.
I shook the redrock hands
in rock shops and coffee stops, one-pump stations
weathering and wilting in the heat.

November, I crossed the scarred ancient fields,
the high plain
where history is unwritten.
Night was the skirt of a woman,
my dark mother,
her cool indifferent fingers.

Winds sweetened by snow
gusted down the Great Divide.
On the bones of a bridge
        I stopt for a smoke
where the single track of the stream
stretcht out unmoving
a hundred hundred miles to the sea.
But it will rise.
Rise and continue
and wind down like a life winds down,
and peter out
at the foot of some coarse gnarled knot of grass.

Below, bobwire in the moonlight.
It gleams and winks. I think
        of Old Gabe,
Bridger and the Bozeman Road,

fenced,
gleaming,
where the great dark herds
had plunged through steep snow
beneath this same sudden moon.
The frozen streambed ambles up
toward a weightless aspen stand.
A sexual darkness beckons
        from beneath their white, white hem.
How much of a man, I wonder,
is snow, is cold,
pusht into driftings by the wind.

Outside a bookstore in Denver
a bum begs a quarter,
eyes so heavy
they rise only to fall, mind
a wall of hard snow heapt against the wind.
And from the window behind,
Bigfoot,
half up-raised, climbing up
out of the snow,
head in rags, mouth agape, hand opening:

BIGFOOT IN DEATH
WOUNDED KNEE BATTLEFIELD

I look to the beggar.
A thousand tipis fill those eyes.
& snow is falling.
& smoke rising, wavering.

In antique clapboard towns,

14

in whitewashed haciendas,
mudhuts reeking of vermin,
(I cannot say it)
in musky old cowtowns a century late dying
the lame bootheels resound on the wooden walk!
I belong to weather-eaten faces.
I have taken from these lives
the stink of livestock.
I measure my height in hands.

And the heroes of the RCA,
ghost-like, crossing and re-crossing the continent
as though knowing
    "who we are"
    "where we come from"
the one word
and no one to tell it to.
I feel the chill snow blowing in
through a broken basement window.
Ice on the creek has melted,
and old, the clouds drift down it
to be buried in the woods.
Last patches of snow dissolve
even as snow goes on falling,
and coming across the field
    I hear a meadowlark sing,
sing its fractured country song.
In foothills a tired old hawk
goes home to scruboak and redrock
having thrown down its hunger in the henyard.
I have forgotten the names of desert flowers.
Cereus. Prickly pear. Is it
loco weed or abraxas?

No one any more
travels the highway in daylight.

In the Big Piney
rivers are ending or beginning,
towers leaning over head
where the pine-scented breeze
    sweeps down through a canyon.
Dogs pant circles in the hills,
and deep in the west
    the same old hawk
hangs curious in the sunset.

They came here first
    a century ago,
pushing up the Missouri in keelboats,
grim wifeless men
    packing pemmican and jerky,
leathery liminal figures
at nation-edge
entering the last great wilderness,
the long glacial streams and natural hot springs
mapped in their faces.
    & I who
have no frontier,
no unmapped regions to escape into,
drive through the Tetons with tourist directions!
I, too,
small in my knowledge of myself,
what song,
with what song
serenade the stooping hawk, call down
the skinny shy coyote, "Old Lobo,

Old Relic,"
I, too, prowling timberline,
belly full of hungry, mouth full of dry.
If Hugh Glass were here today
he'd bust out, I think, those glassy panes
and burn the buildings down.

And where the old cars rust out,
along the Escalante,
shells along waterless coasts, shells
crustaceans have died from
at the bottom of drained seas,
Jackson Hole to Dead Horse Point
on a case of beer & pint of bourbon :
I was a boy here
when I was a boy . . .
        the old man had thick fingers
and rolled Prince Albert from his can.
Like dust, their lives settled down,
a lone grim syllable
repeating itself :
"to survive another season"
the dry wind cracking poetic billboards
that tell them what to want,
dry wind
where their lives and their cars rust out,
that sows their dark seed singing.

The eyes of their children
are empty windows of houses abandoned for cities
when one and one
the farms began to fold.
They carry only their small up-turned palms,

open, empty
as the places where their lives began.
In beer bars, Saturday night,
the men feed quarters to a Wurlitzer
which over and over
repeats their three-chord lives.
Sundays at the whitewashed church
the wife and kids
        hear Brother Albert Smith Walker
tell how his grandad
"came over the hills with Brig Young"
how they weathered that
"first grim winter"
and after Service, ambling down Main,
Ma windowshops
and the children are reflections in the glass.

The ruined stones plead mercy from the plowshare.
Last birds months ago
crossed the grey fields,
the switchback ridge to the south.

When I've nowhere else to go,
and it is too late,
too late in the frozen year to turn back,
deep in crackt ice and crusted snow
I dream the winter away,
dream sun, sky,
belladonna
blooming its delirium
far along the plain.

The dark-skinned alchemist

18

draws figures in the sand.
I cut fences and let my scars speak for themselves:

    Dear Earth,
    Dear Star-crossed Lover,
these words will be all you ever hold of me,
though they change as you hear them, change
even as I speak them,
but they shall be all I ever wear
against this harshest season,
nor will they ever be
enough to keep old bones from their disastrous singing.
Let the Old Ways lie dead.
May the herdsman wrap against his winter.
May stones conspire against the plowshare.
Dreams empty themselves
of themselves
as we empty.

In this season
visited in ice and hunched under old snow,
curl me in rich skins
to slumber through winter.
Mad, gone in the head
and half dead,
I'll shiver down that ancient dream
to toss up old wanderings
in the memory of last year's spring.

II

I AM waiting. Waiting in the hills
patient as a hawk.
Below, the holy city
where the holy men have walked.
A thousand years ago,
a hundred holy cities back,
these men called me Tartar,
Vandal, Arikawa, or Hun.

'was Andy, an old fighter
with a mad woman
who showed me my thirst for blood,
who took me the first time
to the edge death has
when you hold it in your hands,
who gave me the sweet kick and dizzy roar
of a last earthward plunge
and spew of feathers in the air.
And I lay awake all night
on damp ground shivering in my bag,
lay smelling milkweed and the night.

And years later,
on a battlefield in Asia
for a reason I never knew,
shot through with the fever, locked
in a clenched fist of pain,
I dreamed that hunting night again.
    I was young then
    and wrote poetry.
    O I was the sleek interpretor!
    Lorca played my Pound's Flaubert.
    I was irascible and oblique.
Along the damp Asian streets
whores poured from the woodwork
opening coats and thighs,
thieves divided my money while I
divided my life.
I wore a grim, forlorn disguise.

    "Dear Sam:
    Between death's entrance
    & life's easy lies,
    it is poet
    is surveyor of alibis."

Said another: "There are other places
which also
are the world's end."

And I write back: April
is the cruelest month, the old creek
up the cottonwood stand icy,
too swift to freeze,
snow still heavy on the bank,

but rainbow and fat browns
if you find a still-pool
and set a spell.

In the half-froze cottonwood
and aspen logs
lay termites, slugs,
and on good days a bait-worm feast
(reds, which otherwise prefer
the dark sewermud
along the brown canal).
They waited to be bait.

And I slept sound in a grove
where the frogpond croaked all July,
and the gnats and skeeters raced.
But the tracks a man spits down
are followed by the trappers
who are followed by supplies.

Now a Lethe-stink hovers over Zion,
over the creek-corpse and bludgeoned land,
a Zion's Christian Mercantile
    where the frog pond lay,
and not a sign of that river
or of that river's flavor.
Asphalt and tin cans.
Bloated on refuse, a strange
concrete carp floats belly up.
Men with the eyes of swamp flies
swarm through its glassy gut.
A rank breath spells dollar signs in black.
"Birth, copulation, and death,"

said Sweeney,
"You'd be bored."Wheels of commerce
grind in the bowels of the lord.

"Dear Sam :
   How much of a man
   must perish, perish
   gracelessly,
   float away from himself in the blight.
   And worse, much worse, it
   is, yes, so very difficult
   getting the news from verse."

Near a wisp of smoke and churning coffee pot
I hunker in the sunset feeling old.
Out of date,
time out of whack,
a small grey bird with battered wings
wheeling over tenement and stockyard,
over penthouse & towne house
and all glory-to-god-almighty
coughing insidious flak.

I hike the shale slide,
two feet up, one back,
climb into my sleep
among the lodgepole pine
deep into the night.
A barn owl mutters
as the night creatures all arrive.
Tomorrow or tomorrow
the devil gets his due.
Who took the last of what the Ute once had,

who steals from me,
steals from you.

I sniff the mountain meadow,
add twigs to the trickle of fire.
Down the valley
tiny cars crowd homeward along the streets.
A great ball of sun slants across these hills,
crosses the bishop's vast desire,
crosses the Kennecott Copper mines,
and gutted mountains glisten in the heat.
Evening fills my bones.
Fire warms my feet. Too tired to watch,
I fall asleep. Faint moon
shrugs and sighs. Dew stands shimmering in the fields.

When the gnats fall silent
a lone duck yaws across the waterway
arching down the breeze.
In dream I am below,
tromping the shallow swamp,
where, at the edge, I stop,
tentatively stop,
look back and go on :

there are things watching this world,
watching fearfully,
as I watch. Beyond the swamp
the mountain lifts its head,
fierce and still as a dying man,
yet hauls itself
up from the stony century
reaching the thunderhead.

25

Half up the northeast face
the eye of the cave peers dimly down as I climb.
And on last legs
I enter that cave, and during the long dance of the flame
the sunset slips away.
And I curl for the night in the belly of the planet.
And in dream within dream
and with eyes not my own
I leave that cave
remembering the swamplands,
the bad water I stumbled out of,
and cold nights I wander into :

    I have sat in my time
    in stagnant pools
    where film began to form,
    where, from nothing, a breathing . . .

I sag into the mire. I drag
myself up
again and again. Open wounds
pull me, dust
for my eyes and flies
planting eggs in my gills. And
I breathe.
And rise up.

On fishlegs, by fin-fur and eye-skin
I manage the jagged inches.
The world lay still in drowsy wind.
Small, improbable, wretched, I plotted.
I found the ways stars burn, I listened
to their laughter. My feet

found ways to move forward,
I armed them with talons,
I learned to understand.
I must make things my own, I thought,
I must have purpose.

Long grasses hid me.
O timidly, I peered!
I shinnied up trees with hounds
panting after. I wolfed meals,
I catnapped. I ran rabbits
and barked at the moon.

And, set to wandering,
wondering,
I stopped on a hill, picked up
a stone, threw it, it was
god in my hand, an ass's jaw!
The armies of the Griefbearer grew.

Hamstrung, thunder-
gripped, I wrench myself awake.
I creep to the precipice.
The moon is sinking in the swamp.
Its dank skirts shroud its secret.
I who see no longer
the things that leave the swamp,
that try for the mountain below me,
I who am swallowed
in the pit of myself,
half up Olympus I am,
stoppered in its belly
like a boat in a bottle!

And wake, finally,
in the nameless hogan
left by the numberless dead,
and sit cross-legged and numb
by the all night fire
gnawing my heart from a cactus flower.

"It is impossible
to break the human heart!"

Dumb moon and raucous stars
leap from the veins of my hand.
O dunes of my bones,
peristalsis of my days,
what fictions
lead me down these herdways.
I have seen the vacant fires
bantering on hillsides in the rain,

have visited
the heroes of the Teton Mythos
and shared the lover, the Fire.
I have tasted that blood-spattered beginning.
And I'll one day
cross the last canyon in the rain,
set fire the stories they make of this life,

and though the wandering of one
through the sundering of himself
be short-lived,
cut short,

down the chilly sailway of the seals

the babes are flaring their nostrils,
the geese are gathering in flight,
and the phoenix unruffles its feathers,
myth at the ready,
planted in its teeth.

III

AND so gave up on that city
and left the city, climbed up, out
from this crawlspace earth,
set foot on freeman ground,
terra incognita hard as mesquite,
and found the free air, the new air
as pale blood hammered down its labyrinths,

and wanted for nothing,
neither "flagon nor woman,
nor for alehouse"
nor for the hermitage cabin in the redwoods
where the Navarro comes down
to kneel beside the sea.
I, who moved herward, *her*ward
over the years, moved out into open,
heard in the hills a thunder,
Whitman's trumpeteers! old Pappa Walt hisself,
straw hat cocked,
shaggy brow and day long sweat,
tromping the hills, voice high,
in fit regalia, singing,

drinking and singing.

    My words lumber off like drunken cubs,
    each syllable
    yowling off through the underbrush.

And build this house of sound,
this home of echo and fable
calling to itself to "come in, come in
out of the snow!" heaving its rhythmical beams
against the iron weather.

The Old Language, that weapon
of madmen and the mind's holy grail,
is employment of *device*
as one devises
means of survival:
To be a sailor, listen to the sea!

The first into these hills, Old Diah, that is,
Cap'n Jedediah Strong Smith
early out
found bear:
    "Come round th bend.
     Dint see th bar.
     Beg'n, it wuz. BIG sombitch.
     Stood thar grinnin.
     Firz thang wuz,
     I hearda others bahind me runnin.
     Tore off half m'gotdamm haid.
     Thar.

    Ol' Gabe sewed me up.

He's shakin an damn near t bawlin,
but I tol'im how and he dunnit.
Restuv'm
dint believe I could make it.
But I did.''

Old mythical boneyard, old country,
who remembers now. The old sheep's head mountain,
old windings of the river, Escalante,
red canyon, red plain,
THIS is the possibility : the promise you made me,
Mother Country,
and it's not my hands, but my memory loves you,
not my mouth is hungry for you
but my mind,
        America, I see your bones
lovely in the heat,
parched, broke down,
and I hear your calling,
your desperate hard-earned sorrow.

  (September 7 : woke this morning
   to a lone Canada goose
   loafing southward in the wind,
   called out as it passed,
   scrambled after, up the canyon
   through thick box elder stand,
   up dry creek to box canyon head
   where I found a shack,
   wood soft as a lady's hand
   windows in pieces on the floor,
   evidence of magpies in the refuse
   and a whippoorwill out back,

33

planks torn out,
their ashes in the woodstove . . .)

I am who you left me, Mother Country,
who you left me,
"and damnd fine men they was,
Will'm 'enry Ashley's men, alluv'm.
We's tough, we's young,
and shit,
we knowed it wdn't last."   (ca. winter '77)

Rumination. I am given to this
archaeology, though the bones I unearth
be my own. Bear with me, I
may be getting to something, say
the moon compels me!   It's hard labor
a man accepts when times grow lean.

Up the Truckee, late one September,
when the wagons broke down,
running out of food, thought
they would make it over the top,
ate their dogs,
ate their mules,
and the snows set in.
They ate their dead.
(The words live still
though the deeds do not!)
What we have is what we work with,
circumstance
defines necessity. Pound
quotes who? dogs
bark only at strangers.

Was frauds and imposters wanting empire,
possesseurs and schoolboys,
John Fetterman,
CAP'N John Fetterman, the Seventh's finest,
said, "Gimme eighty men
and I'll ride down the whole Sioux Nation."

Sent his saddle home.
Phil Kearney or the Mekong Delta,
it's no difference, call it
Ben Wa, dildoes for the Saigon ladies,
or if it was your mother come dragging in
with scars on her belly, withered breasts
and a bastard brat in her arms?
"Everything's for sale, m'boy!"
What governs best governs least,
is *machine* : must be catholic,
small c, has
to do with judicious.

"What makes peace is bodycount!"
The conception is
peace made, not
what is interfered with,
efficiency measured
in overkill, to the tenth power,
is,
finally,
language,

      of market,
      as market maintains *balance*
      of power!

and Ol' Ez up'n "re-invents"
the antidote : "when the root be in confusion
NOTHING will be well governed"
(Gary speaks "what is to be done")
and when Gabe Bridger
saw Hugh Glass mawed by that bear,
grisly,
and couldn't get off a shot,
he left Hugh Glass for dead.
What a man turns from is what a man turns *to*,
and this virgin land (we called her then)
she was guttersnipe,
street urchin when we found her,
spoils of war, we took her home
and shared her skinny body.
She was young and lovely, lithe,
a Lilith,
something of a siren :
her hills called us up, her rivers
whispered music. And now we wake,
wake cold and spent
to a hag bed-ridden, an
"old bitch gone in the teeth"
and yet love her,
faithless these many years,
we love her.
      And Kenneth quotes : "if thee
does not turn to the inner light,
where will thee turn?"
and a philosopher
at California's finest
asks why poetry need cost so much.
It costs.

36

And when the rains begin
I weep, I throw my hands up
and lie down in my vanishing tracks
and fill my hands with beginning.
When I begin to starve
I strand myself in the snow.
I am beaten and I know it.
I go over and over all the old trails.
Vanity grows thistles which I eat to survive.
My own imagination
howls for my bones in the dark.
The voices that called me
I turned from,
everywhere I go I am recognized,
there is nowhere
else to turn.

Eyes, dreams, lips, and the nights pursue me,
moon in its third house,
and I in rags beside the cabin fire,
wind, moon, and Orion's belt:

    19 May
    Dear Sam, This is not
    really a poem; It just looks
    like a poem Just like you Look
    like a poem, In fact, like
    many poems Held together
    by a belt That says UTAH . . .

Dearest M—
thunderhead yawing down the Los Padres and
it rained a bit last night

37

but today it's dry again.

Strange birds
rise through my blood, Olson's,
"of green feathers, feet, beaks and eyes
of gold" and even as Maximus before me
addressed you, Glou'ster, your gulls
sweeping the bay, even as the good doctor before me
continued his gentle reminder,
which of us, who among,
shall captain his own vessel
in time of peril? who shall call
each man, each woman
proper,
by given name? we are many
among so many.
          More than few called Ezra liar,
more than few called Glass a liar.
More than few invested years
wanting only to disprove them.
But Glass and even Ezra
had other scars to bear, though scars,
scars can deceive,
even the men who wear them.
A man was not made to endure, but to live.
The good, like the Sioux, leave only
the shabbiest of graves
and temporary marker
because it is true after all
that only the winds are forever;
but even as the mountains shimmer,
high sweet air a profusion! even
as the lilacs and lillies-of-the-valley break!

light dazzled
over the emerald tundra,
even as the pale beaks
dip in the frigid water,
Heron Fisher, forefather,
I shall remember :
the wet-heavy breasts of my bathing lover!
the dull brown dust on the road in summer!
the sheep and white-faced Herefords
adrift in that emerald sea,
the quaking aspen behind them
quaking in the breeze,
the old house crumbling atop its knoll
among the mountain peaks,
and even as the peaks await me, light beckoning,
I will pause to remember :

        America,
when the wars are over,
I am coming home;
when the steam whistle sings again in the Rockies,
I am coming home;
I am coming home with meadowlarks beside me,
riding the flatcars, keelboating rivers,
"and THEN went down"
down to the lake in birchbark canoe;

I am coming home, crossing Berthoud Pass
or crossing Loveland Pass,
coming home to Fraser,
down the steep nor'westerly slope
through heavy lodgepole pine,
down a doglegged canyon

onto a doglegged high country plain,
Fraser in the twilight,
trains in the timbered distance,
out of sight,
    clackety-clack, clackety-clack
ticking off the years;
men bedraggled, crossing
the stubbled summer fields,
diesels on Colorado us 40 and going nowhere fast,
(I'll sit this one out)
women dog tired over the stoves
pushing back a strand of hair;

I have come home to years and years ago,
to Turtle Island, to Nordamerika, to
where you were;
where you go wrong is where I get off,
in the high country,
last light of day.

And if you come for me,
come in the moonlight with bourbon and tobacco,
come take your place in your past,
and me and Glass,
Jed Smith and Zeb Pike,
we'll tell you what you *want* to hear,
and only then
I'll show you the photograph,
old, brown,
battered at the corners,
the daguerreotype
of a man
standing beside his word.

BOOK TWO

Solstice West from Tao

I

AND if I were the end of it,
I would not be bitter.
Time ties us deep, deep in its iron clutch;
concrete and carved stone
displace me,
but I shall have sung my song.

And if I speak
of imaginary beings
who inhabit long towers of unnatural, un-
earthly light, if I should say
dark winters, hungry hours
or speak
of a "bare thread of moonlight"
it is gods I mean,
gods we found too easily,
too easily charted, those for whom
we made streetguides of our sins, whose
presences we charted with blue and yellow pins,
and,
if they be gods, let them be wood,
or grass, or granite,

and run cold as rivers run,
they be magick, intact or broken,
unless I be mistaken,
they be meat eagle and the old stomping ground.

I was not mean. It is said
I was mean, it is said I fouled
what I could not eat.
I fouled.
Something to dream on and come back to,
something to return to;
but I killed not,
but for hunger, for self-
perpetuation; I had no sport, no
games for Chance to play.
Gods of high places
are pragmatists all, they worship leisure;
I curled long nights in the bramble thicket,
and came always to a trudging,
trudging down the days.
And I was no martyr. Alone,
mindful, un-
disturbed by the sweep of mountain stars,
I am no martyr.
The white wolf of lightning
strikes fear and I tremble.
The hawk is freer, the bear
more awesome.
Let woodlands be my dynasty,
waterways my maps;
and when they are no more,
when the last tree saunters down time to doomsday,
the last hill sold for lots

and the gaunt birds sing again never
nor carry their hearts to the highlands,
I will have lived the end of it
and I will not be bitter.

Where pathways of the herds had stood,
the dogwood lays out its beauty in the solitude.
A terrible time, a century
before this murderous century,
there were hard women
who wore that hardness outward,
women with hands
like rafters open to the weather
and hearts white as wood sorrel.

    "That ol' woman," the old man remembered,
    "full o' wrinkles she was,
    and mean with scars,
    but'er spirit was *gen u wine*"
    (and he took a spell to say it)
    GEN U WINE
    "an this bare nekkid soil
    was soul enuff f'her,
    huh!
    'Better'n wages, Pa!' she'd yell,
    and I'm sure she's by gawd happy
    with her withered bones beneath it!"
    and under a wooden cross
a mark of her own making,
but it aint that way namore,
it aint that way namore.

But even at the end of it, even

as we mourn the dead and the lost,
we will not be broken.

Call me skunk-bear and nasty,
nostrils flared slightly and eyes in my nose
for looking into wind!
And this roily old river, deep amber,
heavy and slow, but it rises,
I swear it! rises to my singing,
and together, singing one to another,
we cannot be broken.
We have our rite of passage,
listen!
the gods are laughing,
the old hotai of the hills is laughing.

Old Whiskey River lies so still
that days lose their time,
wind loses time,
where the great stars are drifting.

Once, the heroes here were mighty in fiction,
but before them the river ran;
now they are come and gone
and still the Whiskey's running,
still the tall grasses shining in the sun
where furred lives go furrowing.
Time and the river
and wind in the jimson weed
where the high arcanus tundra
is what it is I call *I*,
where I endlessly wonder :
magick is wormwood or sheep sorrel

down among which falls a breathing,
and I listen : I shine like the stars!
it is September and everything is new,
the forest in the rain,
black earth shining,
the dogwood shining in the rain.

The old country is suddenly new again,
made new,
nose clear of fume
and without greater sound than the few squabbling birds,
or water falling over stone.
Somewhere between marshgrass waving
and the dark wings rising,
between thunderclap
and CRACK ! of grassfire burning,
I shall be stalking. O bonfire! flower
of blooming darkness
shall bear up my name in smoke!
My script is the stone-cutter's script,
the hammer and chisel
and ceaseless tattooing,
is one measure : the eye for particulars,
the ear
for a notion of strict proportion,
the memory cloistered, the carved image
upon carved image,
totemic, clearly,
and down corridors, among labyrinths
I've never entered,
are the tea rooms and anterooms
where the totem animals home.
Totem anima : the fish mother,

47

the shrieking ravens of my veins!
here are my feet of sod,
my green-veined hands,
fire and water like any man,
with eye like a windchime turning!

In dream we appear and reappear.
In dream we are, forever.
And in dream or half-dream
I was Hugh Glass,
robbed, stripped, and stricken,
left naked for dead
miles west o' the broken fort,
miles nor'west
of the gnarled scavenger camp-curs
of the Kiowa;
and it was eye and ear got me through, it was
the chant, enchanting heartbeat,
it was Spider Woman, Old
Coyote Grandfather,
words of the Wolverine, a totem
got me through.

    "Only the dark of self is dark," he said,
    "the only dark
      is dark of mind's eye . . ."

and I crawled, hearing it,
singing it over
in idiot monotonous stutter
until I saw the savage eyes of my country
and spit out those faces
and it fell like brass

on ears of falling stone.
We have filled kiva with dung and darkness,
the air with our ashes,
two hundred years in the wrong direction!
thrown up cities like vomit
and wrapped our child
in the robe of anonymity.
We bathe in our saccharine kisses.
And all the while
the Hydra we call the heavens
black star that it is,
falls in,
consuming itself! Narcissus,
God of Man!
and I go in darkness,
where there is no clear line of demarcation,
like old Gabe went up,
into the Tetons in the rain,
and he was out three days
with a Cheyenne scout,
lost, he said, and hungry
when old Gabe give'im hell.
And the old Cheyenne, he
grumpt and sit down—
to chaw a little pemmican,
make a little fire, hunkering,
and says, finally,
"We aint lost.
Camp lost."

We have been to the glass mountain
in hell's back acre;
we stood upright

49

in that strange shaft of moonlight,
that shock
of recognition; and it was cold, o
it was cold
there on the glass hill
without blanket of darkness
so small and so mortal.
When we called out
our cries broke
on glass ears far away.
We all have entered those cool glass rooms.
We could not die there.

Lord of Creatures,
I see spread out before me
the flickerlight of all my days
and they dwindle.
The lickflame melts into hours.
I have seen my name scribed down
in the black book of departures.

(And M has written today
of mint under tentflap!)

In starlight
across some drenched forgotten plain,
in ashes of drowned November fires,
I glimpse among spark and charcoal
the after-life of bison
or of Kiowa.
Among the bare stripped juniper
and manzanita root
are old dog trails and horse trails

lit up
by smatterings of rain
along the migratory roads.
Like this ragweed fire
wet with rain
I smoke and cackle,
"Sweet fire of self," I sing,
and free myself
of myself
in the fire.

And up the black moraine we regard as future,
song weary, weathered,
I lie dreaming,
humming in the wind
like an old guitar
with all the strings unstrung.
And if that be the end of it,
I shall have had the better.

II

A DAY things we did not know were missing
came home to their places:
dread
to its toe-hold in our sleep,
the lean ungulate called autumn
returned to the leaves,

great aunts we never knew we had
uncover themselves in fading halftones
of the Great Depression
in an unimaginable trunk, forgotten,
in an attic,

whole families
we never knew we had,
children in raincoats in the desert,
frocks and elaborate beards
arriving at a station.
All the old tried ways of survival.
A day ashen and still, a day
time returned
from its long sleep in the glass bell of summer.

And the rain falling softly in the mountains
is an old tribal song
someone is singing in oblivion,
the old patchwork earth
is worked and reworked
by a hundred generations;
and the rain in the valley
is a few stolen kisses
planted in the dust.

I have placed my candles
out on the creek
in cottonwood bark canoes
and sent them softly sailing,
out, outward,
against the iron horizon.
Up in the redrock it is said
a man can hear in the wind
the voice of a woman singing,
or in thunder the echo
of hooves on canyon shale.

There are arroyos here
above which even the drifter hawks
have yet to unfurl a sail.
Old-timers have it
that once
the great herds passed here,
grazed the steep canyons and drank deep,
that the grass was tall then and plenty,
but the Old Ones,
the Old Ones have stories
that hang like a mist in the rows,

they, the beaten ones and broken
who have death's palsy upon them,
death pulses in their souls.

    Or Carleton put it :
    "To keep them in line,
    their spirit must be broken."

and no more is their language spoken,
though the spines of their fires
rise from the mesa
straight up
through the long, the windless months,
one and one,
sober and onely,
spines of sulphur and ash
and burning of dry tears,
    "llanto,
    llanto y muerte,
    ardiente"
in a dying land
the living dead
have forged a grim tradition;

    Piedras, Neruda,
    piedras para su llanto;
    Sangre de codicia, Vallejo,
    sangre de guerra, Federico,
    de codicia,
father by son in the rain,
father
by son
lying in the rain

on the blood red ground
a hundred generation!
la casa de las flores en ceniza.

Sombre de sangre
and it came to no good, it comes
never
to any good,
the hatchet forever bloodied,
and all in the name of what god, in
what good cause,
god in all his wonder,
dead men riding down the rain,

el fuego, y llanto y polvo,
cuerpos de aceros asesinados
when the bluecoats came :

    "Columns arched between days
     like the sun;
     who took what they wanted
     and fouled what remained."

—With eyes dry as weathered wagon wheels
the old man surveyed my bones.
His jaw worked up
and down
like a Greek with a mouthful of stones,
then :
       "Gone
     the turn of a single moon
     I came home to the ruin,
     Old Woman stooped burnt sienna

weeding these sad patches."
Bad land scarred her face,
and bad land cracked her hands,
but in her eyes I have seen her memory roaming:
it runs the mesa
in red royal sunset and in sunrise
beyond the battered house and dirty children
who play in the ditch beside it.
And she sings "Soledad, o soledad
my children,
soledad y luto y muerte,
real property is NOT private,
go out with Coyote
to be his nephews and nieces,
taste cactus flowers,
and sing, SING for your power!"

Old Woman knows all the songs, has still
the heart of a hawk,
though, in the firelight
her face is a palimpsest
upon which
all her odes are written.
See how she gapes, how
she shuffles!

    "The Way dies slow
      on the Bosque Redondo.
      My children dead
      in the First War,
      my grandchildren
      in the Second."

Her pearls are kernels
on a bit of string
around a child's throat.
I have seen her cane her way among the rows
with the moon in the Ponderosa
and all the children long departed—
who shall say,
vanished or grown—
and long since even the moon went down
I have heard her chanting,
Old Woman, Mother of Masawu,
mother of Death's spirit,
chanting,
Talavai, kachina of dawn beside her.

It will be said
my Madonna is ugly, beat and old,
but see, see how soft
the skin of her fingers in the firelight,
how
in all that age
the eyes remain alive,
and to me she sings,
she sings of Mangus Colorado coming in,
"O ancient one, proud,
and spoke
of lasting peace
for all people,
and came under truce flag
and against advice from his own people—
Mescalero will not dishonour the world!—
but there are sprouts
that do not flower, flowers

that come not to fruit,"
and she was there
when the bluelegs brought him in,
brought him in
and threw his truceflag in the fire,
"laid him in the dirt,
heated fixed bayonets
in the fire,
put them
to his legs and feet &
AND, when he raised
to an elbow,
shot him.
Boilt the flesh from his skull;
sold his scalp; sold
his skull to a museem back east;
but 'e was better dead than on the Bosque Redondo!"

And when the bluelegs
brought her in,
they put her in hell-on-the-Pecos
where she died the spiritual death
of Carleton's Bosque Redondo.

And they burned out her corn
in the Canyon de Chelly
and they burned her pear tree down:

 "It'as ol' Rope Thrower,
  Eagle Chief Carson who dunnit.
  An' it'as fr the money 'e dunnit."

Give me, O Lord,

the cactus liquor,
give me the greeny pulp
of this dry season,
I'll make a cactus liquor
and pull down those clouds
and sing your praise in the rain.

But O Lord,
sing me no more of sad songs,
sing me no sad songs tonight;
the ache of ages settles in these bones,
the ache
of false starts and missed
directions
settles in these bones.

Lord of Creatures,
Lord of Hosts,
I hear her
sleeping the glass sleep,
remembering the long ride up from the coast—
"miles an' miles of Nevada," she said,
and at a fruitstand
in Santa Clara
selects
a pear
"though they're not as sweet any more"

and in Salt Lake
the streets were bare black slabs,
air rising off them like blisters,
and all her old allies
in hovels on the avenues

with needles in their brains.

Sometimes,
I remember in the night
when cold fills my bones
and heat is less than heat
and I sing the Penance of Heroes,

sometimes,

I remember
all that westering and wintering
and retrace beneath the snow
the old footpaths
across the gouged arroyo,
Dread Mesa,
below the Sangre de Cristos,
blood red! in the sunset, o
in the sunset,
light snow, snow
and a wisp of smoke
and all those winters between us.

Dawn and twilight
I have seen her,
thigh deep in the azure pool,
splash her breasts and face,
throw back her hair,
and laugh, laugh
like the water at her knee.
What ruin! what ruin
we come to, Lord,
what villainy

sheathed itself in my silence!
What held once
all of beauty in its arms
kisses now
the mouth of a carp,
hugs twigs of commerce to its breast,
and sings no more
in winter solstice
the songs of Iitoi,
the songs of power.

III

THEN speaketh the
Lord of Hosts, saying,
"Consider ye,
regard thyself, creature,
and consider the vine, thy brother,
the ewe afield,
as thyself even,

and call not
upon Lord of Hosts,
you who lay havoc
to my chain of composure,
slay the ewe and scatter the bones
and dry up the river
that the vine wither!

Go thee and consider!

And
call for your mourning women,
send for cunning women,
and,

let them make haste
and take up the wailing
and scatter the tears of your children
to earth's end. Go thee
and consider."

We are confounded, confounded
greatly.
Because we are forsaken
the land
our dwelling
cast us out
and grew desolate
and burned red
from the spilled blood of quarrelling
and salt tears
of this bitterest season;
and death has come to the windows,
its palsy fills the sod shacks
and robs our men of their women,
carcasses of men even
fallen like dung in the field.
We are confounded, Lord,
because we have forsaken land.

And with eyes of a witness animal
I came on the Sangre de Cristos,
saw them
bathed in pools of azure light:
they have a psalm for the singing,
dressed in nightshirts of snow,
I've seen them kneeling.

Nor be this Elysium :
I lay three days
face up
in the old adobe Freedonia, Arizona jail,
hung over all the way from Kaibab,
and the Old Man says, "Dammit!
Keep him for all I care."
And I knotted my hair,
went up the high place,
Ge-hennah,
and raised my bloodcry there.

And the bones I wept for!
the scrapped relics
of a past I never owned,
the cleaned and marrow-sucked
indications, pre-
dictions of this life or of
another.

    "Chiefs of the tribes were chiefs,"
    Old Woman said,
    "though the tribes be sundered,
      the wise men wise by *virtu*,
      having learnt
      to look the heart in the eye
      to speak that tongue precisely."

Deer at the salt-lick
are pack animals for piety;
the litany of the wind is divine;
the Fox, my brother, muses, praises
quietude as the clouds roll in.

"Weigh well your words;
   find equity;
   see clear, hear well,
   as the lobo who
   got free also."

(Sd Kung fu tsu,"Worship
the virtu of ancestors, not
ancestors themselves.")
The sun crawls off me
like a tick from a dying dog.
How do I go on.
Old coals fading out,
camped beside a forked gouged stream
petering out in a netherworld
of lost worlds I think I can remember;
I almost *can* remember
to before the blood-splashed thirst set in, yet
it must be only wounds I remember,
violets like bruises, the
awful rose. Here is my cup of coals, a
supper of testament :
what we do not know will betray us,
do we not speak of Old Pike,
Zeb Pike,
the man who saw never
the peak which carries his name?
Or in the Yucatan
the three turistas
slung heavy with cameras, . . .
maps, lenses, souvenirs, postcards,
and the whole goddamn country
out of sight.

"lenake waku wapi kte!"
chant the Teton tribe : all men
move with a purpose.
How pungent the coals
after a rain in the mountains!
In half-sleep I hear I think
in the leaves
the One, the Perfect,
the no-name of us all
as the first star
stutters open.
All people move with a purpose; all things,
with a purpose.

And down slowly
from their blue glacial remote
I have seen our bad forebears
narrow and mean with desire,
the cold ones and bitter.
And I have chipped this out in petroglyph
across the cavern wall :
Remember, my child,
how the rains pour down,
pour across all the forest,
yet merely seep through the ancient thicket;
in the life of one man
is room only
for the incense of a little fire,
a few scattered ashes, perhaps,
but no room at all for desire.

Be always, my daughter,
of all things,

be of the earth and be prize
for no man, no, be
no man's trinket! Nor be
less fertile
than standing fields
nor sharpen your appetite ever
upon the whet-stone of wanting,
and may your hands be stained forever
and your lips
by the blackberries and elderberries you gather,
and wear proud
the calluses of your planting;
Lord of Hosts is lord
of all seasons
sure as woman is mother of man;
be one,
be always
the witness animal,
see/hear
with your heart
what you can;
and remember the solstices, the times
of planting,
and learn the river-magick,
how in the rain one's breath
collects into rivers on the pane;
and listen!
silence is the laughter
of the hotai of the mountain,
and not even the steady mountain,
nor glacial stream,
but only all-humbling mothering seas
shall run forever!

and as Jeffers went up Point Sur
and Tor House went up,
awesome,

and Falcon Tower,
Roan Stallion steady as Lobos Point,
strong against tides,

be yes
a thing
of nature, not
man apart, be green
as the girl with seaweed in her hair,

and remember old Cawdor
though he be less
than the Boswell of Musketaquid,
lord knows, he aint Thoreau,

remember old Cawdor
for his own fierce beauty,
power raw, so raw
he was his own undoing!
the man of Falcon Tower,

and when the wind is thick in the eaves
and the night heavy,

know in your heart the stars are,
lightly,
and lie still then and consider

this prayer,

and be then my child,
creature of the earth
and for.

BOOK THREE

Longhair

I

"BUT you'll one day
have to get up
and leave the dead, leave them
where the dark blood of this world
draws them under,
walk away from it all,
enter the air like ether, opening
like an horizon peeled into sunset."

Listen.
The one we call Too Late
rings his black hammer in the rain.
I lie still
hot in the April grass.
It crawls across my skin.
When I tune my ear to the ground
I hear a heartbeat there.
Despair lies down beside me in the dust.
"I'll do what I can," she mutters,
"I'll do what I must."
She opens her robe
and shows me all her wounds.

73

A word I cannot utter
carves a niche in my throat. And yet
I know
I'll one day get up, press
these few bones a last time to my breast,
weep again perhaps, but kick up dust
from here to where my footsteps end.

On the Plain of Lost Tribes
I scent again
an animal in the wind;

I lie out prostrate in the April bake,
lie out like a house built of bones
cracking the shins of the wind.
Seven days I swoon
baking my brain in the heat,
seven days
lost to a world I almost remember again,
and the Dead put on their faces in the fire
and the Dead come home again.

    "Man's no better'n his tools," Ott said,
    "nor tools make a woodsman of a fool."

And old Ott had a hatchet,
"Had it twenny year," he said,
"put on half dozen handles
and wore out three heads"
who at seventy
still could follow his heart's desire
"without overstepping the T-square"
who gave me a saw

with half the teeth broke out,
like teeth from abused tongues he'd said,
who showed me his teeth
in the bottom of a water glass—
"Got na bite wi'out'em!"
and smoked the meanest damn cigars
in a back porch easy chair,
his step on the gravel drive
was Billy Buck's on the bunkhouse stair
when I was leaner and young.

And the Dead
strip off my flesh
and scatter it
in the Valley of Affliction
as I swoon deeper yet.

Man's no damned better'n his tools, Ott said,
who used an axe
like a butcher a boning knife,
each tree felled, precise;
now Otto Empey's dead
who, tired,
stooped to flowers, that old man,
bandana at his hip,
"I sweats a deal," he said,
thumbed in a bulb, and
flip-o-the-wrist
and covered it again.
Not a damned bit better, Ott,
as I remember you :
standing there, cigar
between thumb and fuck you fingerstub;

and I wondered even then
where missing fingers went,
what they may have found without you
in this crack or that,
in dark ore,
pitch belly of that mine.

And the Old Ones count my bones
when I am dry of flesh,
meat empty,
and summon my loves,
and one for each bone,
and scatter my loves,
and one for each bone, . . .

Somewhere, I think an axe is falling,
falling through hot April air
across the arid plain
where even the trees sag down
to grovel on their knees.
It is Otto Empey
cutting down the hard dead prune,
suspect,
in the outback of my days.

Lord, the drought of March has passed,
the drought of April is upon me;
all mortality draws up its knees
and leans its weight on me.

Downwind
the children of god, blessed in their valley,
through scrub oak, through thistlejack,

across the foothills beyond.
A fat woman in a Winnebago shack
eases her haunches
into her easy chair.
She shifts her ponderous weight
from hip to hip, settles,
barks orders at her brats,
and flips a TV on.

Across the plain, morning
of the seventh day, on winds
sweet with carrion, the music
of Mastambo I hear,
sparrow hawk on slender wing,
curlews of foxtail,
finches darting over
to roost in the chaparral.
An eagle with iron feathers
and with bloody iron beak
skulks, scowls,
and paces a bleeding bough.
I ascend a tall smoke tower.
The world below is amber
and bathed in hues of grey.

Across the far dim bluff
dividing then from now
the old Outrider
reins in a dapple mare.
He wipes his mouth
at his shirtsleeve and reads
a spine of dust. The Crone
had cried : "Across

the next hill forever
where the lowlands lie in the heat.''
He dreams a western sea
and rubs his blistered feet.

Who leave no trace, though
etched into each face
a thousand miles and more,
generation,
the Old Man with a dungfork in his hand,
Otto Empey in the damp black shaft
twenty, thirty years,
a Jonah in a landlocked whale,
or Glass, the thrice-born,
forty-what-years-old
and crawling, who vanished,
or Tom
Broken Hand Fitzpatrick, that son-
of-an-Irish Drinking man
who left Hugh Glass for dead,
absconded with his blade,
braggart and drunk

and outriding the road to Oregon.
With moon upon the olive bough
I crack an ancient eye :
I get up
with these old bones inside me bleating,
take medicine shirt, take up
the Chant,
and wear a scarab in my ear.
I load this life once more
upon that overwrought travail,

pass through the gateless gate
where nothing is obscured,
pass among birds, pheasants
in corn stubble picking, light of morning
licking at my feet, wisdom of the dead
unbroken! Otto the venerate
as much in this heart's beating
as in the dark drift of earth
which drew him under.

And the children come down grey
to the dusty country station,
train come and gone,
gone all the way to doomsday
when the dark hills fall into night
and the clouds blow back
the scent of evening lilacs
and all the simmering girls
take off their magick rosaries
and paint their lips and nails black.

Is only the wearing out of a way
just before an age is over,
old names for things impaired,
casualties scribed down
on the ancient bloody palimpsest,

was only
the wearing out of a way,
sundering the old order,
children at the curio
'cross from the station
and the weeds thrust up among ties

all down the track,
whistles forgotten by the smokestack
and all the souvenirs on sale.
A boy with money in his jeans
holds up his bandaged hands
to gesture toward a ring.
Nothing is what it seems.

When undulant tall grasses
call me into dance
the flesh takes on
"the pure poise of spirit,"
as Roethke put it, and tall winds
wander over stones, old cemetery,
old town vanished around it,
Poose and Otto Empey
among the stones of Zion,
lichen-flowered fields undulant in the wind
early weeks of summer or late weeks of summer,
and no one stoops again.

Girls in Sunday ruffles, the fear
of god in their breasts, the Lion
of fire belcht salvation, the black stud
of damnation whinnied in the wind
where no black man ever
put on their magick alb,
and I
who exalt a hell as much as any heaven
lay down my bones in the heat.
The whole of heaven
shook down its light
and gave this world to me.

The far torn station
wilts in the white white heat;
a lone wren ambles across the street;
the blind man in Temple Square
waves pencils in the air; while high above
simmering in the waves
in a suit of solid gold
Moroni tonelessly plays.
"I loved a girl with sunrise in her hair."
"I loved a girl with evening in her hair."
The amputee in Temple Square
waves shoestrings in the air.

And Kenneth had said
they were healthy and happy, said
they were in the most
"peaceful city in the country, maybe now
in the world"!
and death is napping in the orchard,
the sun sleeping lightly
on the bare backs of sleeping women.

That is NOT love
is passion
which is greed.
And the old man went unwanting,
made not by greed, but love,
and dies the death eternal
in a high burning valley
known to some as Zion.
Who feared no god
nor man.

II

WHO drift north
under the Great Bear
in waters of the minotaur,
makers of war over Helen,
makers of poems over Helen,
north by the golden calf,
heroes of war over land,
heroes of Furies, lovers of,
whose ghostly beauty burns:

discharged body half sunk in the stinking eddy,
blood in the irrigation ditch, corpse
a hundred feet away;
mantles of mourning gone up in smoke,
candles of mourning blasted into flame;
the babe asleep in its crib,
a plastic cannon in its paw;
the old dog gone under the heels of the highway;
the pig-farmer's boy
from Ioway City
who left his legs at Cho Sen;
the grocer's kid from Moline

sent home in a plastic sack;
the intern with magic hands,
out of Missoula mere months,
blown out of his boots and through a plaster wall;
the lovely child of Nashville
whose ashes were scraped from her car;
the bishop's boy in Brigham
with brimstone in his teeth;

HUMAN VOICE!

what drone of blood, what black
epiphany you pray to!
The People burnt their dead,
hung up their legends in the huts,
banners of smoke, ciphers
of smoke and water
whose every tale
held a knot of human gristle in its teeth.

I will say they were young,
I will say
their deaths were not deserved;
I speak here plainly of the losses,
whose song is stripped of voice,
nor hands shall ever touch
the gaunt shroud my heart shall wear.

But you the living
will be well-cared-for;
you will be told when the waiting war is ready;
as for myself, I go north,
north by nor-west to the sea,

north until stars
are far away as miracles I believe in,
and I hear the lull, the
plaintive litany
and listen when leaves moan and trees
tremble like girls in the shadows.

The Old Woman, ripe with child,
bore down her fruitful pain
and when the water broke
the birthshriek struck the air
with pathos, dis-
belief! like cries
of sealpups slaughtered in the icefloe.

And if, rising or falling,
they make a circle of stones
and kneel low
and lay low their eyes
as eastern tribes are wont to do
as if in prayer
when the sun rises or sets
or the moon is hollow or not at all
or at equinox
when the light across the world falls cruel,
it is not stone we pray to,
but the rude imperfect image
of ourselves, lovely
though imperfect, a kind of song
(O lovely, and imperfect!)
as the rose outside the sill is,
which, opening,
finds too late it cannot open endlessly,

surrenders to taunts of wind,
each petal let go
in the manner in which
a man lets go his life, slowly, or
a woman lets go her children
into lives,
song like the rose imperfect,
desert-thorny beauty, dirges
for the losses, litanies
the exact fabric of grief, psalms, cadences
the rhythm of sweat or of salvation,
HUMAN voice! weakest instrument,
sad unharmonious chord,
what shriek or groan, what
parcht, dis-
ordered scale, this song, chimera,
till death is the legend of sleeping women
and salmon-spoor the only hand of time.

Pittsburgh : three boys
open the cold cadaver;
rude entrails
spill across their hands;
"She will be opened and inspected,
certified in minutes"
and mounted in a limousine.

Because the face of death is green
they will not see death's face;
their hands go grey.
Pale to the bone,
death is the constant companion.

Cold moon rising in Chicago
like a tracer in a Gatling gun;
la mirada de la muerte es verde
and smiles in the spring;
green death on brownstone streets,
ivy upon walls,
yet somewhere far away a music
through lightly veiled sills,
the fair city drones on.

Delicate fern in that far garden now,
small rose of which Williams might have spoken
budding and pale in old coffee tin
or in chipped vase, row
upon row
and delicate white crosses
planted in that lawn;
I lift my eyes to old roads
and blue rogue rivers,
let others look back on Sodom!

Enormous beauty in that land.
I have news of the homeland:
another war in the South,
and women in the fields again
and autumn on the wing.

Equinox.
But news is slow coming,
we know not what to believe.
When we look to that country of the heart
we look east
to white-haired toothy peaks.

Years and years have marched between us,
and now a war in the South.
Soon they will bury the king.
Already the women harnessed, already
the mules afield, and yet
there is beauty, there is,
how say it,
sweat and pathos, each face
a note from a distant horn.
The Elders speak religious upheaval,
boys and women
retain a nervous silence,
and the men make leather sing
against the polished steel.
We wear our cool Castilian eyes.

And beauty though it be, heavy with sorrow,
agonizing grace, that old basalt of the blood,
icy unsavory grace.
Constant in crises, we wear our gritty glamour:
skin of hammered copper, hands of painted clay.

And now the old road winding down
beside the dusty riverbed. July,
and the journey neither joyous nor
broken, keeping to paths
we find with heart in hand.
Dust on the bones of my pony,
dust on the riverbed.
Dark tracks working off the trail behind me
up the wind-torn hill.
When again I see the torn adobe,
the sun-tortured wood,

I live again in the bones of the fathers
and work again
like a widow. When the tall bell
peals in the village
I disremember the season of its sorrow
and reason for the weeping;
I go heavy as a riderless horse
come home again too soon;
you carried your hearts like guidons;
you were no more real
than the smoke from last night's fire, a moth
about the flame
beating my lips with your wings;
I held you like the wind,
the sheer dream of you, cool fingers
pressed against my throat, your breath
that blackens my spine.
I would have named you
Not-My-Own,
and called you another country
nor understood a word.
Your black tears tacked
to your doors like hides
are nothing to me now;
I would call you that other country
and hold you like light in my hand,
your ciphers of smoke keeping secrets with the trees,
ripe blood holding back its dark equation;
a dog of the mountain,
I bark at my shadow
riding forward on the rivulets;
in cold dawn the icy pawprints
circle my cabin door. Now and again

a horseman drifts by
beneath Orion's belt.
This world goes naked, strange and wonderful!
Your god was Ares,
Isis, mine.
I wear a shitbug in my ear.
Even now
there are wet leaves clinging to your hair.
You who have warmth without comfort
have life without living;
it is cold where you go.
You sing like the bird
with the broken wing, like wounded dawn,
like a spiked rat you sing.

And writing this at night
after seven months of rain,
cutting firewood in the rain, or clutching
the coffee cup to my breast
and warming prat against the iron stove,
it all comes back,
cool Olympus over the fog, green, hazy,
snow upon the mountain,
January cold,
and a small craft lilting in the waves,
and the one back there, bent, working
not for wages, but love of labor;
and over the vast soft water
no whitecaps break; reft
of breakers the inland sea lies still.

Tree and I go down the hill
wrapped in lowlight fog

to spend a few coins on beer.
Kenneth'd said, "Sexual love
is one of the most perfect forms
of contemplation!"

I stay up all hours, reading, smoking
marijuana, scribing notes to myself or
beginning letters I've no inclination
to send. When the clouds break up
and sunlight wanders over,
we stack wood, clear a little space
in third growth timber.

Writing now, after thirty years of rain,
what moves magnificent, in masses, yes,
"careless of particulars"
—old treemonger crow
defaming his stately madrone,
red moon
        up from the mainland
midafternoon;
        the girls of Cadiz
are dancing!
        to the man with the silver hands.
Red moon ascends
        to a balcony of wind;
Crow and I have nothing;
he covets a tired madrona,
I wear gold inside my smile.

III

AND so it was
Bill Ransom went to it,
tearing out alder and salal,
second year growth and deep in slash—
"man cd tear'm out by hand
        he'd a mind to"

and tore out a couple to make his point,
and tore out growth from a buried logging road
and laid up his beam-logs to dry 'em.

And driving back over the hill,
bluegrey town slack on its hill
a mile or two away,
the lone boat silent on the green grey water
under the low sky
and not a wave on the Sound;
or sails up but not enough wind to fill them.

Down alleys of cedar
and alders heavy with swallows,
the clear air alive

with hum of big cats pushing slash
where the dark blue chimney,
the burn :
    the rhodies so thick,
the alders so thick
the spruce and the fir can't survive them,
and the SCREE, SCREE, of the crows
long after sunset
and swallows mating well into March,
swooping and diving, alive
to the music of living,
but the gov'ment went to it in Asia,
a cruddy little war—
just a few million in ashes—
but Critter wouldn't go,
the swallows wouldn't go,
nor the crows abandon complaining,
proving Critter's much sense as a sapling,
and Old Bob wouldn't go
and he served a year in Portsmouth,
and Randy wouldn't go, he served
a year in Safford,
and Dave Harris wouldn't go
and he got two years
in Texas
while senators debated the value
of continued burning of Asians,
raised taxes and their salaries
and the level of human misery :
there are men with the yokes in their hands!

So long ago now that no one cares to remember,
and still, the burning of Asians,

the blue chimneys
of Asians burning,
and the Professor from Californey
inquires : "Re— the chinoisie"
meaning J. Masao Mitsui
while fools in petroleum suits
take notes on 'creative potential'
and still the Asians, dying.

Water bluing this morning, clouds
white as leghorns.
The cowards who went there
came home full of needles, creating
a petty scandal;

the Old Man, his veins
so weak he taped them,
scarcely controlled his anger.
"There are men with the yolk in their hands!"
"Men begin wars
who can't put up a decent hen roost"
and in those bent peasant shoulders
are dreams of sunlight in morning
through their fingers
and small wands rising through the water,

and Pardee went to it in Jughead green,
and there was *I* in a stupor,
and he found his blue penumbra,
first day, patrolling
in Cambodia,
and he sniped a sniper in the back
and he fell in the mucky paddy,

not dead,
the clean hole through the thick of his shoulder,
and the lieutenant comes up
as Pardee's about to shoot him,
and the Looie grabs his piece,

rolls her over,
the bullet through her then
through the babe in her arms,
and the Looie left them face down in the paddy,
and now he remembers the green,
and you can't hear them crying
for the sound of the counting of money—
blue fingers of rain
falling through the jungles
half the world away,

and blue on the Sound and nary a single sail,
nor a whitecap,
and the sleepy village
sound asleep on its tail
while fire falls through the rain,
or fog hugs these hills
tumorous in the blue,
and not a car on Water Street
and old Gunn's market finally closing down,
forty years,
and the building sold from beneath him,

but you can't hear him crying
for the sound of the counting of money,
who don't know their shade from their hue.

"Mosta them kids was cannon fodder!
Shot'em like ducks in the water."
McGrath writes"labor and place,"
the long afternoon of the onion,
Spanish in its grace,
the chiseled corn
implying a nobler race.

Dark-before-dawn, a spear of grey blue
straight through the thick cicadas,
what-ever's become of that country,
the miles and miles of bobwire
and softly waving horizon,
wheat-weaving winds all across Wyoming,
frosty in September
and steaming all summer, streaming
meadowlarks before the derricks came;
now all the way up from the Gulf
the one-armed bandits plunder,
driving needles through her
to suck up all her veins;
she was a country in the country of the stars.
Train came straight through her,
annihilating herds.
Till even the dead Salt Lake
creeps back from the stinking city
wishing death to the golden spike.

The Old Man spits tobacco,
"Couldn'ta donner worse
she was a whoreson's daughter!"
(The Professor lately acknowledges
the poverty he's come to:

he lately condescends
to peruse old Ezra's *Cantos*.)
The Big Machine gone mad,
the poem, the man said,
is a made thing,
reveals only in proportion to its tuning,
is a *made* thing;
the government at best
a gov'ment of words,
and that wry Gros Ventre/Blackfeet
with fine old eye drove out
beyond the Little Big Horn
where lawns are sober as links
and he asked the hired hand there
if he might picnic with his Lady
and the guard says, "Hell no!
This here's a monument
to Custer's Seventh Cavalry."
and the upstart buck says, "Shit,
guess we had our picnic
a hunnert years ago."

And where lay old Yellowhair
with his head cleanshaven
and with a woman's blade in his chest;
where drunken Grant
but sleeping off eternity;
and where the old Rough Riders
in iron jocks with all their buckshot smiles.

And,
where's that bastard Andrew Jackson
but burning slow in hell.

Deep into the west
the humpback fluteplayer
plays the sun to its grave.
The green world pales in eve's crimson,
Isis translucent in twilight,
crimson falling through water
as though it were glass,
y la luna de sangre,
third house and clear,
illumined by mid-afternoon
and with blue heavens shining through it
and the starlings settling,
stilling the alder leaves
as the beetles begin their drone,
and the oarsman
glides slowly into blue,
muscles singing,
and the woman at her loom drops a hand
to begin her evening weaving
as the green corn
leans toward the sea
where crimson like blood whorls through.
And the sun is rising in Asia,
the darkness gathering in pools.

And I am old and growing dim
and remember the last time,
the Old Woman,
Scots/Papago, half-breed and tribe wise,
she had down a mule deer,
tied at the haunches,
big ears stiff up, eyes
wide and bloodshot

as she splinted the foreleg
wrapping the tendon
in a cold wet skirt
and her hand so shot with arthritis
that she three times lost her knot;
the yearling doe, three legs staked
and Old Woman astride the other,
rolled her eyes from side to side,
bucked her head,
and the old woman cuffed her.
It went on that way for an hour,
and Old Woman ground her barley mash
and went out to gather her apples,
and the god-damned doe
laid right there and died
like what was broke was her pride.
But Old Woman never spoke, she never once
mentioned it. And all that night
the dogs were up,
whining under the porch or skulking
around the yard,
and the fire burned low
and lent its light to the woman :
her eyes lightly closed,
lips parted
and with the tip of a tooth showing through,
and her lower lip moist
from her tongue's sly maneuver
as she rocked beside the fire.
I heard her to hum, I thought,
and listened hard :
only the chuckling of the fire.
She tamped her little pipe

carved from the mesquite stump,
tamped down her "green tobacky"
and struck a match at her hip.

  .   .   .

where the San Juan River
turns off toward Mexican Hat,
fifty-five-or-six it was then
and the old man had a brand new wagon,
Ford,
four doors and big v-8
which I'd hotwire weekends
sneaking out at night
and when I botcht the job
the ignition melted away
and I stood the old man off with a bat.
The night holds sway.
And sick to the bends,
a hot pint of creme de menthe
and some Mason jar tokay,
red stains all down my shirt
and sicker'n a dog with the blight,
went down in the new mown hay
half shit half dirt, blind,
and skidded to a halt.

And Old Woman cleaned me up,
though she threw that shirt away.
Once, her eyes were turquoise,
her tongue cool silver.
Shunned among gossiping twits
and stranger to the market place,
what could she live but the life of quiet labor,
sunrise and sunset

and long wandering field,
red clay aflame with evening
and the warm red sand on her toes.
"This country don't grow miracles!"
she'd exclaim,
and naked 'neath her light chemise
with July on the high plateau,
she'd move from tree to tree
bending low,
splashing water from her pail,
caress each budding petal,
press her fingers to that soil
she'd hauled by the bucketsfull
up from the long dry well,
and in those days she'd three good dogs,
sheepers from the herds,
and one had a light blue eye
and followed her everywhere,
a husky bitch, bobtailed,
that strutted like a stud
and kept her nose in the air.
And with her own two hands
she built that shack
atop her half-a-hill
with dogs underfoot
and the scent of sage all April
and desert birds eddying slow in the air.
She spoke no tale of Coyote,
though she planted a painted corn.
And Jesse Bemer lay in the flatbrush
all one summer afternoon
for the queen of Dead Horse Point
to draw her evening water.

And when the sun went low
and the mesquite shadow long,
she dragged out her wooden tub
and stood it in the sun;
cool water, four buckets, and she dropped
her chemise and shivered
though the air was warm
and she turned, sensing he was there,
and gave him her profiled breast,
slow,
languid with her hands, head turned,
"just so,"
and her hair piled high 'til it came undone,
and she turned once more
to show her silken back, long crimson
caught in mahogany hair.
And when he breathed she caught him,
and hung a tooth in his ear.
And the winds beat Devil Flats
near forty years
while Jess got grey and leathered
and she braided silver through her hair.
And the blue wash of pinon
and gnarled juniper
and blue La Sals rising like smoke
over redrocks mesa, over yucca,
mesquite, and prickly pear,
and she sent me down a thousand feet
of solid Wingate sandstone
to find a petroglyph
and all that vertical length
the oxides, manganese,
wove desert varnish into blueblack

desert veins. Then the Money Man showed up
and built him a Little Riata
and mined uranium
and fostered a tourist trade.
And she's no more than memory,
whose blue veins were carved, bone
by bone chiseled through the years,
but the little shanty still is sound,
though the walls a little grey with weather,
and shingles flap against the wind,
the windows webbed,
and the floors never tire of complaining.
And Jesse's handmade forge,
where he laid his ham-like fist,
till he fell four hundred feet
to the roily Colorado;
they never found his body
and they never found that mare,
though a ranger got part of the saddle . . .
and she went twenty years beyond him
in the same old pick-up truck,
doing the same old seasonal labor,
and no less of beauty, though aged
into a crone, and wryly watched
the treaties signed
that parceled off the land,
"Bad half o' two nations! Likely
I'd give a damn!" Or,
"Landownership's no issue
where there aint a drop o' water!"
and I went north without her,
following the tundra wind,
long northern, where they'd put

a price on seals, claiming they
wasted fish, four-bits a head it was,
and the sealers cursed the landsmen
who broke out power rifles:

"SONSABITCHES DON'T EVEN PELT'EM!
Take a fuckin headskin
and leave'm right there freezin!"

And Old Woman
listened as I told her,
and stared at the floor past her knees,
her knuckles turning snowy
on the arm of her rocking chair.
And the village that year
moved up to Monticello,
and on that bank
the Phlegethon ran dry
where Geryon's ghost cried out
and the fruit of avarice was sown,
avarice deep and wide,

and when she wouldn't sell, their curse
ran deep and wide;
nor money move her, nor gold
persuade her.
So they waited, they
waited her out.
Whose blood lies still in that land.

EPILOGUE

And that was the country,
steeped in legend,
still as the Sleeping Woman,
a dream vision,
the redrock of her marrow—
where Carleton slit her tongue,
where Rope-Thrower sucked her dry,
the Hag-of-Forked-Tongues speaks her lie—

to he who makes gain
from labors of other men
the lie is spoken;
"what is not done well
        by the hands of one
is done poorly by the hands
        of the many;"

and to he whose calluses rejoice,
        the invention of the fields :
the land yields—

where a man honor the Word
the Word
delivers justice.

                40072—77

This book was composed Monotype by Scott Freutel at the Spring Valley Press. The text is 12 pt. Italian Old Style, designed by America's premier type designer, Frederic W. Goudy.

The book was designed and printed by Tree Swenson & Sam Hamill on a hand-fed Chandler & Price platen press. The paper is Rives buff. One hundred fifty copies have been sewn into cloth over boards by Lincoln & Allen of Portland, and signed by the poet.

The paper edition is printed photo-offset from the letterpress original.